MW01265466

Like Pure Gold

The Story of

LOUIS G. GREGORY

written by Anne Breneman
illustrated by Gregory Newson

BELLWOOD PRESS
Evanston, Illinois

Bellwood Press, Evanston, Illinois 60202
Copyright © 1998 by the National Spiritual Assembly
of the Bahá'ís of the United States
All rights reserved. Published 1998
Printed in the United States of America
00 99 98   3 2 1

Library of Congress Cataloging-in-Publication Data
Breneman, Anne, 1943–
        Like pure gold : the story of Louis G. Gregory / written by Anne
Breneman ; illustrated by Gregory Newson.
                p. cm.
        Summary: Describes the life of Louis G. Gregory, the grandson of
slaves, who became a noted and well-loved Bahá'í, or follower of
Bahá'u'lláh's teachings.
        ISBN 0-87743-704-1
        1. Gregory, Louis G.—Juvenile literature. 2. Hands of the Cause of
God—United States—Biography—Juvenile literature. 3. Bahais—
United States—Biography—Juvenile literature. 4. Afro-Americans—
Biography—Juvenile literature. [1. Gregory, Louis G. 2. Bahais.
3. Afro-Americans—Biography.] I. Newson, Gregory, ill.
        II. Title.
BP395.G73.B74   1997
297.9'3'092—dc21
[B]   97-9451
                        CIP

                                                                        AC

"He is like unto pure gold.
This is why he is acceptable in any market
and is current in every country."
—'ABDU'L-BAHÁ

Dedicated to the many children of South Carolina,
who have a "destiny before God"
at this moment in history

*L*ouis George Gregory was born in Charleston, South Carolina, on June 6, 1874. His mother and grandmother had been slaves on a plantation in Darlington, South Carolina, until they were freed after the Civil War.

When Louis was five years old his father passed away. After some time his mother married a kind and good man named Colonel George Gregory. Colonel Gregory accepted Louis as his own son and made sure that he had a good education. Louis loved and respected him.

One terrible night a mob of hateful white men attacked Louis's home and shot his grandfather. These men were sometimes known as the Ku Klux Klan. Because Louis's grandfather was a successful blacksmith and was able to buy a mule and a horse, these men wanted to stop him. They didn't think that people who had been slaves should have the right to live happy lives as free citizens.

Louis's grandmother helped him to understand what had happened. She thanked God that the hateful men rode away without killing other members of the family. She had a narrow escape because she refused to show any fear of the men who killed her husband.

Louis knew that his grandmother was very brave and hoped he would be brave too. A full-blooded African, she was a very strong influence in his life. She was loving, generous, and God-fearing. She taught Louis to love, pity, and pray for those who are sick with hatred. He never forgot this lesson.

Louis's grandmother also showed him how to find humor even in the most difficult situations. He often heard her warmhearted laughter in their home.

*L*ouis's childhood was full of hardship. He often thought about his father and grandfather and missed them. His family was poor and worked hard to make sure that he and his brother had clothing and food. Louis worked too. His stepfather sent him to a tailor to learn how to make and mend clothing after school.

In spite of the hardships, Louis dreamed of getting a good education. He wanted to help make the world a better place for all people to live. Louis's mother and stepfather saw how much he wanted to learn and encouraged him to save his money and study his lessons. They sent Louis to the first school in Charleston open to both black and white children.

Louis learned to work and plan, sacrifice and save, so that his dream would come true.

*S*oon Louis began studying at a private high school for African Americans. This was the Avery Institute in Charleston.

When it was time for college, Louis did not have many choices about which school to go to. In those days, an African American could get a good education at only a few colleges in the United States. One of them was Fisk University, and that is where Louis went. He happily graduated in June 1896.

This success was only the beginning for Louis. He wanted to be a lawyer. There was only one school where African Americans could study law, and he was accepted there. To study at Howard University, he had to go far away from home and work harder than ever. He got his law degree in March 1902. His family, especially his grandmother, must have been very proud of him.

oon he was practicing law with another lawyer in Washington, D.C. He became very successful and was known by many people as a good man and a good lawyer.

This success was surprising to many people. In those days many white people thought that African Americans were not as intelligent or capable as they themselves were. Separate public bathrooms, water fountains, hotels, and restaurants were made for white people and black people in many towns and cities in the southern United States.

Black children and white children could not go to school together. They had to go to separate schools. In many parts of the country white men and women could not marry black men and women. Often African Americans who were able to overcome the difficulties of their lives were attacked by white men who did not want them to succeed. Some of them dressed up in white hoods and called themselves the Ku Klux Klan. The hooded men would try to scare African Americans by setting fire to their homes or by lynching black men. After all, this was how Louis Gregory's own grandfather had died.

In Washington, D.C., Louis Gregory was known for his peace-making ways, especially between Northerners and Southerners. He helped them become friends. Many people noticed his sincerity and friendliness. They also admired his serious mind.

One white friend told Louis about the Bahá'í Faith when he saw how interested he was in the unity of the races and peoples. At first, Louis wasn't very interested in this new religion. But he soon saw that Bahá'u'lláh's words could solve the problems of the world. He became an eager student of the teachings of Bahá'u'lláh, the Founder of the Bahá'í Faith.

When 'Abdu'l-Bahá, the son of Bahá'u'lláh, heard about Louis Gregory's deep love and reverence for Bahá'u'lláh's teachings, He called him a "Wooer of Truth." He knew Louis admired truth very much.

Though 'Abdu'l-Bahá lived an ocean away, Louis could feel His shining love. At the beginning of June 1909, Louis Gregory decided to give his heart and his life to Bahá'u'lláh and to the spread of His teachings.

He wrote to 'Abdu'l-Bahá and asked for permission to visit 'Abdu'l-Bahá and the holy shrines of the Bahá'í Faith in Haifa, Palestine.

Many years earlier, Bahá'u'lláh had been exiled from His homeland of Persia. He had been sent to the worst prison of that time, in the prison-city of 'Akká, near Haifa. 'Abdu'l-Bahá, a young man then, had gone with Him. When Louis wrote to 'Abdu'l-Bahá, He still lived in the prison-city of 'Akká.

People from the West wanted to visit 'Abdu'l-Bahá to learn about the teachings of Bahá'u'lláh. Louis was invited to visit in 1911.

*I*n the Holy Land, Louis asked 'Abdu'l-Bahá what would happen to the black peoples of the world who had suffered so much from the prejudices of white people.

'Abdu'l-Bahá lovingly promised that, as the black and white peoples began to learn of Bahá'u'lláh's teachings, they would come to love one another. He said they would even want to marry one another.

He told Louis that Africans had once been great peoples and that he should "be a leader to them" and "Guide them to the Truth."

A woman from England named Louisa Matthew was also in Haifa visiting the Bahá'í holy places at the same time.

'Abdu'l-Bahá spoke to Louis and Louisa separately while they were in Haifa. Then He brought them together and expressed His wish that they should marry. He said this would help to bring the races together in harmony.

Both Louis and Louisa knew how difficult this would be. Many whites were against the marriage of blacks and whites. In many parts of the United States, such marriages were against the law. Another problem was that many blacks were afraid and suspicious of whites.

When Louis was leaving the Holy Land, 'Abdu'l-Bahá told him, "Go forth and speak of the Cause of God. Visit the friends. Gladden their hearts. You will be the means of Guidance to many souls."

ouis and Louisa admired one another's good character and dedication to the teachings of Bahá'u'lláh. They wanted to please 'Abdu'l-Bahá. Soon after returning to America, they married and settled in Washington, D.C.

*L*ouis and Louisa spent the rest of their lives spreading the teachings of Bahá'u'lláh. They traveled to many places to help the Bahá'í community grow. Louisa traveled in Europe because she knew many languages. Louis traveled all over the United States—especially in the South. Unfortunately, they were unable to make many trips together at that time because of racial prejudice.

For a time, the Gregorys even lived in Haiti to help establish the Bahá'í Faith in that country.

Often Louis was without money and had holes in his shoes. But he always looked and acted as a gentleman. He was courteous, patient, friendly, and long-suffering.

He was welcome in many towns, churches, schools, colleges, and homes. Sometimes, though, he had to go in the back door of a hotel where he was to be the speaker.

'Abdu'l-Bahá was so pleased with Louis that He wrote, "I hope that thou mayest become . . . the means by which the white and colored people shall close their eyes to racial differences and behold the reality of humanity." 'Abdu'l-Bahá hoped that Louis would bring white people and black people together so they could be friends. He also encouraged Louis to rely on God, no matter what difficulties he faced. 'Abdu'l-Bahá told him that he could gleam and shine like a star in his work to guide and unite people of both races.

That is exactly what an eight-year-old girl saw when she met Louis. She first noticed the beauty and peace of his face. She was walking home with him after an evening meeting. Then, when she looked up at him, she stared in wonder. His dark face on that very dark night was glowing with light. Just as 'Abdu'l-Bahá had said, Louis Gregory gleamed and shone like a star. She couldn't take her eyes from his radiant face.

One day in 1912 when 'Abdu'l-Bahá was visiting America, a special luncheon was held in His honor in Washington, D.C. Important diplomats and government officials were present.

The table was set so that each guest was made to feel important by his closeness to the guest of honor.

An hour before the luncheon, 'Abdu'l-Bahá sent for Louis, although Louis had not been invited to the luncheon. When the host came to escort 'Abdu'l-Bahá to the table, Louis stayed behind in the parlor.

'Abdu'l-Bahá asked for Louis. He refused to begin the luncheon without him. Louis was then seated at 'Abdu'l-Bahá's right, in the best seat, right next to the guest of honor!

That day 'Abdu'l-Bahá spoke with the guests about the oneness of humanity.

*Y*ears later, in 1922, Louis became a member of the first National Spiritual Assembly of the Bahá'ís of the United States and Canada. He served as one of its members for twenty-four years.

He also continued traveling and teaching others about the Bahá'í Faith, visiting and encouraging the Bahá'ís, arranging conferences that would help black people and white people learn to love and accept each other.

He wrote articles and pamphlets about the Bahá'í Faith. He wrote many warm, thoughtful letters to help people better understand how God wants us to live.

People loved Louis Gregory wherever he went. He was a pure channel for the Holy Spirit.

Louis didn't think of himself first, however. He didn't want to be the center of attention. He was always dignified, humble, and modest.

In their later years Louis and Louisa moved to Green Acre Bahá'í School in Eliot, Maine. After many years of serving and teaching about the Bahá'í Faith in that area, Louis died on July 30, 1951. He was seventy-seven years old. He was mourned by friends of every color, friends from many nations all over the world.

Several years later Louisa died and joined her beloved husband. They have been laid to rest side by side in a lovely cemetery near Green Acre.

*T*hroughout the world people have been encouraged by Louis Gregory's shining example. Schools in Africa and America have been named after him.

In South Carolina, the Louis G. Gregory Bahá'í Institute was founded in 1974. The first Bahá'í radio station began broadcasting from Louis G. Gregory Bahá'í Institute in 1984 using his initials as part of its station identification call letters—"WLGI."

In Charleston, South Carolina, Louis's childhood home has been purchased and turned into the first Bahá'í museum in North America.

Upon hearing of Louis Gregory's death, Shoghi Effendi, the Guardian of the Bahá'í Faith, gave Louis a great distinction. He named him a "Hand of the Cause of God" for his years of untiring, heroic services to the Bahá'í Faith.

Louis Gregory was like pure gold.

He was a true Bahá'í.